GUINNESS ILLUSTRATED COLLECTION
OF
WORLD RECORDS FOR YOUNG PEOPLE

Norris McWhirter and Ross McWhirter have been combing the world for twenty years collecting fantastic achievements, incredible stunts and bizarre marvels of nature for their GUINNESS BOOK OF WORLD RECORDS.

Now they've created a series especially for you! And each book in the GUINNESS ILLUSTRATED COLLECTION OF WORLD RECORDS FOR YOUNG PEOPLE comes with Norris McWhirter's and Ross McWhirter's personal guarantee that every achievement, fact or event recorded—no matter how unbelievable—is absolutely true!

Looking for a "hot time"? "Komar" (Vernon E. Craig) of Wooster, Ohio, had one when he endured the highest temperature in a fire-walk. On August 14, 1976, he walked through coals that were heated to 1,494°F. at the International Festival of Yoga and Esoteric Sciences, Maidenhead, England.

GUINNESS
BOOK OF
EXCEPTIONAL
EXPERIENCES

BY NORRIS McWHIRTER & ROSS McWHIRTER

Illustrated by Kenneth Laager

BANTAM BOOKS · TORONTO · NEW YORK · LONDON

GUINNESS MUSEUMS

- Empire State Building   New York City
- Ocean Boulevard   Myrtle Beach, S.C.
- Clifton Hill   Niagara Falls, Ont.
- Parkway   Gatlinburg, Tenn.
- Lake of the Ozarks   Missouri
- Fisherman's Wharf   San Francisco, Calif.

GUINNESS BOOK OF EXCEPTIONAL EXPERIENCES

*A Bantam Book / published by arrangement with
Sterling Publishing Company, Inc.*

*Sterling edition published November 1976
2nd printing . . . . June 1976
4 printings through June 1979

Bantam edition / September 1980*

Based on the Guinness Book of World Records
Revised American Edition © 1976, 1975, 1974, 1973, 1972, 1971,
1970, 1969, 1968, 1966, 1965, 1964, 1963, 1962
by Sterling Publishing Co., Inc.

ISBN 0-553-13740-9

Published simultaneously in the United States and Canada

PRINTED IN THE UNITED STATES OF AMERICA

0 9 8 7 6 5 4 3

INTRODUCTION

What can happen on, in and around our world?
After 26 years spent collecting the world's most
unusual experiences for the GUINNESS BOOK
OF WORLD RECORDS, I think the answer is
anything!

I realize that some of the facts included in this
book seem unbelievable, but every one has been
checked and authenticated. You can believe every
statement made. Every experience illustrated is
true and accurate.

Norris McWhirter

Swimmers learn to "tread" water with their hands and feet so that they can stay afloat for long periods of time. The longest time anyone has stayed in the water this way without touching anything and without any rest breaks is 64 hours. Norman Albert set this record at Pennsylvania State University, November 1-4, 1978.

Many people have sailed boats down the Mississippi River. Fred P. Newton of Clinton, Oklahoma, used a different method. Between July 6 and December 29, 1930, at age 27, he swam 1,826 miles from Ford Dam, near Minneapolis, Minnesota, down the Mississippi River to New Orleans, Louisiana. He was in the water for 742 hours. At times the water temperature fell as low as 47°F. and he had to protect himself from the cold with petroleum jelly. It was the longest distance anyone has ever swum at one stretch.

In tennis, before the introduction of the tie-breaker system in 1971, a player had to be two games ahead in a set before he could win it. In 1969, Pancho Gonzales (U.S.) played 112 games against Charles Pasarell (U.S.) the longest match in the history of the Wimbledon championships. In the 5 hour 12 minute match Gonzales came back from a two-set disadvantage (22–24, 1–6) to take the last three sets (16–14, 6–3, 11–9) and the match.

Henry L. (Hank) Aaron broke the record set by George H. (Babe) Ruth of 714 home runs in a lifetime when he hit number 715 on April 8, 1974. Besides the home run record, "Hank" Aaron also holds the record for the most runs batted in and the most total bases in a lifetime.

Hank Aaron

Babe Ruth

Before trucks were invented, horses were used to move heavy loads. At fairs, men would pit teams of horses against each other to prove who had the strongest pair. The greatest load ever moved was by a pair of Clydesdale draught horses who pulled 50 logs which weighed almost 48 tons. The horses pulled the logs on a sledge litter across snow at the Nester Estate, Ewen, Michigan, on February 26, 1893. This sort of contest continues even today, but the horses have been replaced by highly modified mechanical tractors.

The largest prisons in the world were penal camps near Karaganda and Kolyma, in the U.S.S.R., which in the late 1950's held between 1,200,000 and 1,500,000 people each. That is like jailing all the people who live in the cities of Detroit or Philadelphia. At one time under Stalin there were almost 12,000,000 people kept in Soviet camps, most of them citizens of the U.S.S.R.

Can you imagine not sitting down for a whole year? Swami Maujgiri Maharij stood up continuously for 17 years, from 1955 to 1973. He did this while performing Tapasya or penance in Shahjahanpur, India. He leaned against a plank when he wanted to sleep.

He finally got his day in court. On April 28, 1966, the longest lawsuit ever recorded ended in Poona, India. On that day Balasaheb Patloji Thorat received a favorable judgment on a suit filed by an ancestor in 1205—some 761 years before!

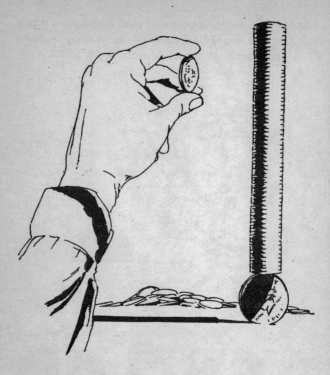

Alex Chervinsky of Lock Haven, Pennsylvania, started his feat of coin balancing with a U.S. silver dollar standing on edge, and stacked 130 coins on top of it in 1974. He had been practicing for 26 years.

The longest continuous session of horseshoe pitching was 130 hours by a team of six playing in shifts in Tucson, Arizona, March 12-17, 1979.

Everyone knows someone who is on a diet to lose weight, but no one is like Paul Kimelman of Pittsburgh, Pennsylvania, who set a world's record for speedy slimming. On December 25, 1966, at the age of 21, he weighed 487 lbs. Then he went on a crash diet of 300 to 600 calories per day— equivalent to 4 to 8 ounces of hamburger. By August, 1967, he weighed 130 lbs., a total loss of 357 lbs. Today, he has stabilized his weight at a normal (for him) 175 lbs.

The beauty contest is an All-American tradition, begun with the first Miss America contest at Atlantic City, New Jersey, in 1921. It was won by a petite, blue-eyed blonde, Margaret Gorman. Since then the contests and the contestants have changed. The Miss World contest was begun in 1951, to find the most beautiful girl in the world. And there is even a Miss Universe contest with entries from 78 nations. Whoever wins that is "out of this world."

A hypochondriac is someone who thinks he is sick, no matter how healthy he is. The worst hypochondriac was probably Samuel Jessup, a wealthy cattleman of Heckington, Lincolnshire, England. From 1794 to 1816, he took 226,934 pills, including 51,590 pills in one year. It is recorded that over the years he drank 40,000 bottles of medicine. Despite his imagined ills, Jessup lived to the surprising age of 65.

The worst reported case of swallowing foreign objects was an insane woman, Mrs. H., aged 42. She had 2,533 objects, including 947 bent pins, removed from her stomach in June, 1927, at the Ontario Hospital, Canada.

If you want to play golf, but don't want to carry golf clubs around the course, just throw the ball. It took Joe Flynn, 21, just 82 tosses to throw a ball around the 6,228-yard, 18-hole Port Royal Course in Bermuda, on March 27, 1975.

How big can a golf course be? Floyd Satterlee Rood used the whole United States as one when he played from the Pacific surf to the Atlantic Ocean. The 3,397.7-mile trip took 114,737 strokes from September 14, 1963, to October 3, 1964. He lost 3,511 balls on the way.

When people lie about their age, they usually pretend to be younger than they really are. But many people claim to have lived for unbelievable lengths of time. The greatest authenticated age to which any human has ever lived is over 114 years. Shigechiyo Izumi of Tokunoshima, Kagoshima Prefecture, Japan was born on June 29, 1865, and was recorded as a 6-year-old in Japan's first census of 1871.

If being old makes you wise, then El Hadji
Mohammed el Mokri, Grand Vizier of Morocco,
was one of the wisest. He reached the age of 116
years according to the Muslim calendar before he
died on September 16, 1957 (that is about $112\frac{1}{2}$
years according to our system). He was the oldest
man ever to be in charge of any country.

What an heroic sandwich this would make! The largest salami was 18 feet 10 inches in length and 28 inches around. It weighed 457 lbs., and was made by La Ron Meat Company at Cosby, Missouri, on January 29, 1978.

In New York City, Broadway is the place to put on a play. Some shows open and close on the same night as "Kelly" did, with a loss of $700,000. Some, though, start with a long run and are frequently revived. "Fiddler on the Roof" (above) set a Broadway record of 3,242 performances. It opened September 22, 1964 and closed July 3, 1972. Paul Lipson played the main character, Tevye, 1,811 times during which he had 10 different stage "wives" and 58 "daughters."

The aircraft with the largest wing span was the late Howard Hughes' H.2 "Hercules" flying boat. It had a wing span of 320 feet, had 8 engines, and was 219 feet long. On November 2, 1947, with Hughes himself at the controls, the plane rose 70 feet above the water as it flew for 1,000 yards off Long Beach Harbor, California. The plane cost $40,000,000 and flew just that one time. It was scrapped in April, 1976.

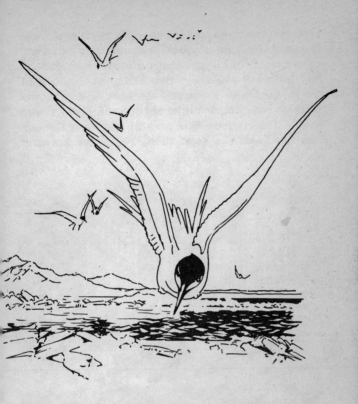

Many birds migrate as the seasons change. The greatest distance covered by a bird wearing an identifying tag during migration was by an Arctic tern. This bird was banded as a nestling July 5, 1955, in the Kandalaksha Sanctuary on the White Sea coast of Russia. On May 16, 1956, it was captured alive by a fisherman 8 miles south of Fremantle, Western Australia, 12,000 miles away.

Like natural fireworks in the night sky, the Aurora Borealis (Northern Lights) are caused by electrical solar discharges in the upper atmosphere near the North Pole. If you live within 20 degrees latitude of the magnetic pole, you can see this display at some time on every clear night of the year. People who live in the Hudson Bay area of northern Canada have sometimes seen them 240 times a year.

This spider may not be satisfied with just the occasional fly. The largest spider webs are those made by members of the genus Nephila. These tropical orb weavers spin aerial webs which have been measured up to 18 feet 9¾ inches in circumference.

C. Fred Ahrendt of Dayton, Ohio, is the most successful treasure hunter in the world, but he doesn't
need treasure maps. His secret is his metal detec-
tor. By August, 1976, he had found a total of 175
class rings (the earliest from 1890) and 179 gold
wedding rings.

Arrows can be shot more than a mile if you lie on your back and use your arms and legs with what is called a footbow. The longest shot ever recorded was by a professional archer, Harry Drake, of Lakeside, California. On October 24, 1971, he shot an arrow 1 mile 268 yards at Ivanpah Dry Lake, California. Drake also holds another distance record using the crossbow.

The longest time anybody has been the head of a country was 36 years, 84 days. Prof. Dr. Antonio de Oliveira Salazar served that long as President of the Council of Ministers (equal to the rank of Prime Minister) of Portugal from July 5, 1932, until September 27, 1968.

The longest reign of any monarch was that of Pepi II, one of the pharaohs who ruled ancient Egypt. His reign began about 2310 B.C., when he was 6 years old and lasted for 94 years.

For an exceptional experience of your own, try saying this slowly, then faster and faster still: "The sixth sick sheik's sixth sheep's sick." This has been deemed to be the most difficult tongue-twister by Ken Parkin of Teesside, England.

Thomas Martyn, a Professor of Botany at Cambridge University, England, held his professorship for a record 63 years, from 1762 to his death in 1825. Previously, his father, John Martyn, had occupied the same position from 1733 to 1762.

A goldbrick is someone who tries to get by without doing any work. Kevin Temple of Alnwick, England, certainly isn't a goldbrick. At Acklington, England, April 30, 1976, he laid 6,429 rough-pressed bricks in an 8-hour shift. He was aided by a crew of 5 men, who mixed mortar and brought up the bricks.

Tom Slaven, of Australia, broke 4,487 bricks by hand in November, 1975.

Man has drilled down into the earth farther than Mt. Everest rises up. A drilling 6.04 miles deep on the Kola Peninsula, U.S.S.R., was announced in July, 1979. The total depth is planned to be 34,450 feet.

A waterspout is similar to a tornado, but it happens over water. The highest waterspout that has been reliably recorded is the Spithead waterspout off Ryde, Isle of Wight, England. It was measured by sextant to be about a mile in height on August 21, 1878.

The highest officially recorded wave at sea was computed to be 112 feet from trough to crest. It was measured from the U.S.S. "Ramapo" as it proceeded from Manila, Philippines, to San Diego, California, on the night of February 6–7, 1933, during a 68 knot (78.3 m.p.h.) gale.

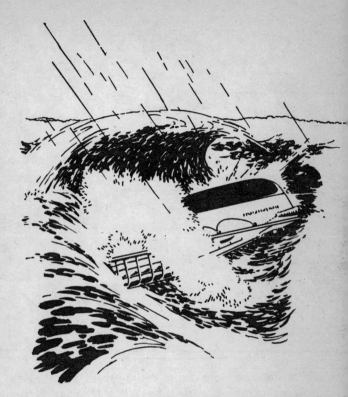

When you go to sea and become used to the rolling movement of the ship, you are "getting your sea legs." No one could get used to this movement, though. The ultimate in rolling was recorded in heavy seas off Coos Bay, Oregon, on November 13, 1971, when the U.S. Coast Guard motor lifeboat "Intrepid" made a complete 360-degree roll.

The earliest solo around-the-world flight was made July 15–22, 1933, by Wiley H. Post of the United States in a Lockheed Vega "Winnie Mae." He started and ended the flight at Floyd Bennett Field, New York City, flying the 15,596 miles eastwards in 7 days 18 hours 49 minutes. He landed 10 times and was in the air for 115 hours 36 minutes.

The first person recorded to have "walked around the world" is David Kunst, who began his trek from Waseca, Minnesota, on June 10, 1970, with his brother, John. John was killed by bandits in Afghanistan in 1972, but David arrived back in Minnesota on October 5, 1974, after walking 14,500 miles.

The longest recorded tug o'war lasted 2 hours 41 minutes. This occurred at Jubbulpore, India, on August 12, 1889. The contest was between "E" Company and "H" Company of the 2nd Derbyshire Regiment of the British Army.

A "moment of truth" can take less time than you might imagine. In a Golden Gloves tournament in Minneapolis, Minnesota, November 4, 1974, Pat Brownson was floored by the first punch of his opponent, Mike Collins. The referee stopped the bout without a count in the shortest boxing match on record, taking only four seconds.

You could catch a whale with this, if you could find a hook big enough. The longest known species of giant earthworm is Microchaetus rappi of South Africa. An average-sized specimen measures 4 feet 6 inches, but one 22 feet in length was collected in the Transvaal in 1937.

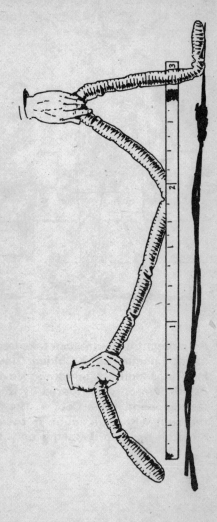

Pity the paperboys! The largest single issue of a newspaper was "The New York Times" of Sunday, October 17, 1965. With 15 sections, and 946 pages, each copy weighed 7½ lbs. It was issued at the end of a long strike.

The space age started with the launching of a liquid-fueled rocket by Dr. Robert Hutchings Goddard (1882–1945) at Auburn, Massachusetts, on March 16, 1926. His small rocket reached an altitude of 41 feet and traveled a distance of 184 feet. He had patented the rocket 12 years previously.

When the spacemen came back to earth, they often landed far from where they were scheduled to come down. The most accurate landing from outer space was the splashdown of Gemini IX. On June 6, 1966, Thomas P. Stafford and Eugene A. Cernan landed only 769 yards from their recovery ship, the U.S.S. "Wasp" in the western Atlantic.

The largest pyramid and monument in the world isn't in Egypt. It is the Quetzalcoatl at Cholula de Rivadabia, 63 miles southeast of Mexico City. It is 177 feet tall and its base covers an area of nearly 45 acres. Its total volume has been estimated at 4,300,000 cubic yards, compared with 3,360,000 cubic yards for the largest of the Egyptian pyramids.

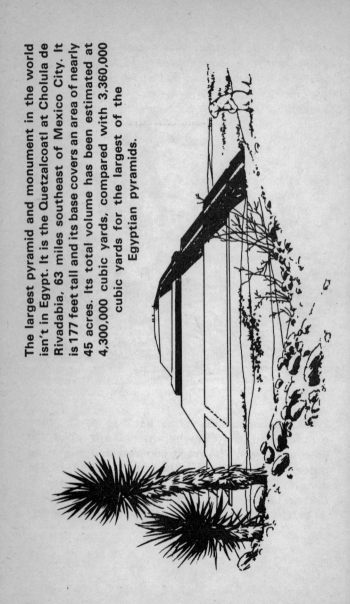

Justice may be a strict taskmaster, but it pays well—to some. It is estimated that Jerry Geisler (1886–1962), an attorney in Los Angeles, in the latter part of his career was the world's highest paid lawyer. During this time, he was paid $50,000 in fees for each case.

The world's most durable hairdresser is Gerry Stupple of Dover, Kent, England. On March 5-19, 1979, he worked for 341 hours 58 minutes, non-stop —cutting, setting, and styling hair.

Do you enjoy seeing the latest fashions? At the world's longest fashion show you could have seen them all. Held at the Roseland Catwalk, Sydney, Australia, on June 16-18, 1977, it lasted 48 hours. During the fashion parade Lyn Snowdon, Kay Hammond and Virginia Conner each completed 41.4 miles on the runway.

Persons able to speak understandably at a sustained speed above 300 per words per minute are a rarity. The highest speed recorded in a public speech was a 327-words-per-minute burst in a speech by U.S. President John Fitzgerald Kennedy in December, 1961.

When two airplanes fight a battle in the sky, it is called a dogfight. The top air ace of World War I was the Red Baron, Manfred von Richthofen of Germany. In his red Fokker triplane he shot down 80 Allied aircraft before he himself was downed in 1918.

Some people claim to be "strong as nails." Joseph Greenstein, known as the "Mighty Atom," was. At the age of 53, he bit a 20-penny nail in half before an audience at Sigmund Klein's gymnasium in Brooklyn, New York. As shown here, he was able to bite a tire chain in half. In his 80's, he was still able to bend steel bars with his bare hands.

Two Englishmen, Mel Robson and Stuart Hughes, have both extended hot water bottles to 5 feet 6 inches across before the bottles burst. Franco Columbu burst this type of bottle in 23 seconds in California, in August, 1979.

Sing the right note loud enough and you can break a glass. Fräulein Marita Günther, who was trained by Alfred Wolfsohn, can find the right one, if anyone can. She is able to sing all the notes of the piano, from the lowest, A'', to the highest, C''''''.

The longest recorded solo singing marathon is one of 134 hours 54 minutes by S. A. E. W. Perera of the Sri Lanka Army, May 8-13, 1979.

Bobby Hull is fast! When he played in the National Hockey League he was the fastest skater, having been measured at 29.7 m.p.h. He also shot the puck faster than anyone else—his left-handed slap shot was once clocked at 118.3 m.p.h. Hull also holds the record for most 3-goal games—28.

The longest-lasting baseball pitcher was Hoyt Wilhelm. Between 1952 and 1972 he threw his knuckleball in 1,070 major-league games for nine different teams in both the American and National leagues—New York, St. Louis, Atlanta, Chicago and Los Angeles in the National League, and Cleveland, Baltimore, Chicago and California in the American League.

The largest bridal wig ever made was created by Jean Leonard, owner of a salon in Copenhagen, Denmark, and is rented by her for weddings. Nearly 8 feet in length, it is made from 24 tresses, costs $1,000, and it certainly makes the bride easy to pick out. An even longer wig, 15 feet in length, was made by Bergmann of Fifth Avenue in New York City in 1975, for a picture in "Vogue" magazine. It is now on display in the Guinness World Records Exhibit Hall in the Empire State Building.

Are you taller than your best friend? When Don Koehler, the world's tallest living man (8 feet 2 inches) met Mihaly Meszaros (known as "Mishu"), who is one of the world's smallest living men (he is only 32⅝ inches tall), the difference in their heights was a record 5 feet 5¾ inches.

Hot-dog skiing includes everything from aerial maneuvers called "daffies," "helicopters," and "splits," to ski ballet. The wildest hot-dog stunt so far was accomplished at Mont St. Saveur, Quebec, Canada, where 21 skiers performed a simultaneous back somersault while holding hands on March 12, 1977.

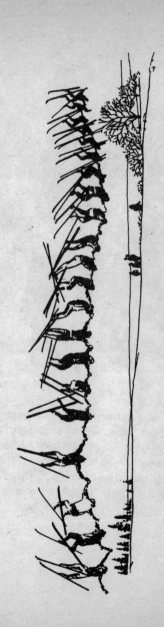

The highest speed recorded by a man on skis is
124.412 m.p.h. This record was set by Steve Mc-
Kinney of the United States at Portillo, Chile, on
October 1, 1978.

The national anthem of Great Britain is "God Save the King." On the morning of February 9, 1909, a German military band played it 16 or 17 times without stopping on the platform of Rathenau Railway Station, in Brandenburg, Germany. The reason for this was that King Edward VII of England—the man whom they were to welcome—was inside a railway car struggling to get into a military uniform and he could not come out until he was fully dressed.

And the hits just kept coming. Harry Lillis (alias "Bing") Crosby, Jr., has sold more records than any other recording artist. Since his first session on October 18, 1926, he recorded 2,600 singles and 125 albums. He received a platinum disc in 1960 to commemorate his 200,000,000th record sale. On September 15, 1970, he received a second platinum disc when Decca Records claimed a sale of 300,650,000 discs.

The longest possible great circle sea voyage can be made by traveling longitudinally (north to south) on the globe. The 19,860-mile voyage would take you from a point 150 miles west of Karachi, Pakistan, to a point 200 miles north of Uka, Kamchatka, U.S.S.R., by way of the Mozambique Channel, the Drake Passage and the Bering Sea. This is equivalent to driving from Los Angeles to New York City and back three times.

The world's loneliest island is called Bouvet Øya (formerly Liverpool Island). It was discovered by J. B. C. Bouvet de Lozier on January 1, 1739, yet no one landed there until Captain George Norris did on December 16, 1825. This uninhabited Norwegian dependency lies about 1,050 miles from the nearest land—the uninhabited Queen Maud Land coast of eastern Antarctica.

How high can a kangaroo jump? One kangaroo cleared a pile of lumber 10 feet 6 inches high, while escaping from a hunter. This set a record. A female red kangaroo, while being hunted, made a series of leaps which included one of 42 feet, to set the distance jumping record.

Today, most cows are milked by machine. In some places, though, there are still hand-milking contests. The record for hand milking belongs to Andy Faust. In 1937, he totaled 120 gallons in 12 hours at Collinsville, Oklahoma.

The longest recorded roller skate was 4,900 miles by Clinton Shaw. He went across Canada from Victoria, British Columbia, to St. John's, New-foundland, on the Trans-Canadian Highway from April 1 to November 11, 1967. On a trip from New York to California in 1974, he skated 106 miles in one day.

The world record for long-distance horse-racing and speed is held by a horse named "Champion Crabbet." In 1920, he ran 300 miles in 52 hours 33 minutes, carrying 245 pounds.

Need help with your arithmetic? If so, you may find this useful. The world's longest slide rule is one of 320 feet 11.1 inches in length. It was completed by students of Alvirne High School, Hudson, New Hampshire, in March, 1979.

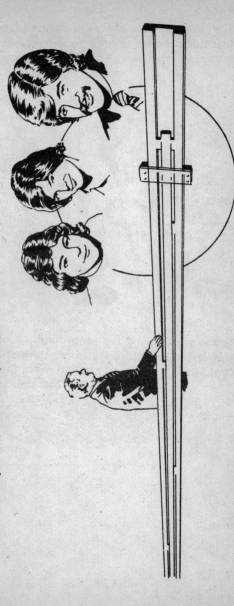

The largest pancake ever flipped intact on any griddle was one 12 feet in diameter by the Liberal Jaycees at Liberal, Kansas, on February 9, 1975.

The first long-playing classical music record to sell a million copies was a performance by Harvey Lavan (Van) Cliburn, Jr., who was born in Kilgore, Texas, on July 12, 1934. His recording of Tchaikovsky's "Piano Concerto No. 1" was made in 1958 and sold 1,000,000 copies by 1961, 2,000,000 by 1965 and about 2,500,000 by January, 1970.

Did you ever hear of "duck tail" haircuts, Butch wax, or the malt shop from what were called the "Fabulous Fifties"? Even if you haven't, you may have heard the song "Rock Around the Clock," which has sold 25,000,000 copies and is the biggest selling "pop" single of all time. The song was copyrighted in 1953 by Max Friedman and James Myers under the name of Jimmy De Knight. (Pictured is Mr. Myers.) It was recorded on April 12, 1954, by Bill Haley and the Comets and immediately took off.

The largest recorded dog litter is one of 23 healthy puppies born on June 9, 1944, to "Lena," a foxhound owned by Commander W. N. Ely of Ambler, Pennsylvania.

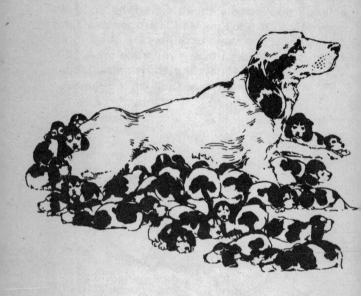

Many people's favorite seafoods come from the bivalve family, which includes clams, oysters and mussels. The largest of this family is big enough to bite back—the marine giant clam. A specimen measuring 43 inches by 29 inches and weighing 579½ lbs. was collected from the Great Barrier Reef, off Australia, in 1917. The shell is preserved in the American Museum of Natural History in New York City, but is not on display.

Do you like to fish? John Reader does, perhaps more than anyone. He holds the marathon fishing record of 504 hours, set at Hutton Pond, Weston-super-Mare, England, August 20-September 10, 1978.

The longest distance surf cast ever reported is one of 1,000 feet. This was achieved on a beach in South Africa. The caster? Name unknown.

Don't mince words with Roy Dean, 43, of Bromley, Kent, England. He holds the record for the fastest completion of "The Times" of London crossword puzzle under test conditions. He finished it in 3 minutes 45 seconds in the BBC "Today" radio studio on December 19, 1970.

The fastest time recorded for "panning" 8 planted gold nuggets is 14.45 seconds. This was done by Lance Murray of Ahwahnee, California, in the 1978 World Gold Panning Championships held at Tropico Mine, Rosamond, California, on March 4-5, 1978.

The world's fastest woman, Marlies Gohr, of East Germany, reached a speed of over 24 m.p.h. in her world record 100 meters. She set an electronically-timed mark of 10.88 seconds at Dresden, Germany, on July 1, 1977.

If you want to ski down from the top of the world, you will need a parachute. Yuichiro Miura of Japan wore his as he skied 1.6 miles down Mt. Everest, starting at 26,200 feet above sea level. In a run on May 6, 1970 he reached speeds of 93.6 m.p.h.

If you want to see the largest eye of any living animal you'll have to get wet—it belongs to the giant squid. The diameter of the squid's eye may exceed 15 inches. Compare that to a diameter of 3.9 to 4.7 inches for the largest blue whale, the greatest inhabitant of the oceans.

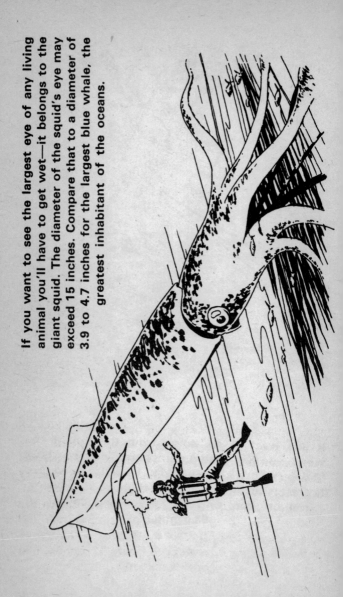

The record descent into the ocean was achieved when the U.S. Navy bathyscaphe "Trieste" hit the ocean bed 35,820 feet (6.78 miles) below sea level. The "Trieste" made this descent on January 23, 1960, manned by Dr. Jacques Piccard and Lt. Donald Walsh of the U.S. Navy. At this depth the water pressure is 16,883 lbs. per square inch and the temperature is 37.4°F. It took 4 hours 48 minutes to go down and 3 hours 17 minutes to come back up.

If at first you don't succeed, try, try, again. Mrs. Miriam Hargrave, at age 62, of Wakefield, Yorkshire, England, failed her driver's license test 39 times before finally passing on her 40th attempt in August, 1970. By that time, she had spent $720 on her driving lessons and could no longer afford to buy a car.

Kitty O'Neil, of the U.S., is the world's fastest woman driver. Driving the 48,000-h.p., rocket-powered, 3-wheeled S.M.I. "Motivator" over the Alvard Desert, Oregon, on December 6, 1976, she reached a speed of 524.016 m.p.h. Her official two-way record was 512.710 m.p.h.

Persistence is its own reward. The world's most unsuccessful but published author is William A. Gold, and he has had only one other reward—a 50-cent payment from a newspaper in Canberra, Australia. This is the only money he has earned after 18 years, writing over 3,000,000 words, including 8 full-length books and 7 novels.

Between 1968 and November 30, 1974, Mrs. Marva Drew, 51, of Waterloo, Iowa, typed the numbers 1 to 1,000,000 on a manual typewriter, covering 2,473 pages. When asked why, she replied, "But I love to type."

The greatest price ever paid for a used car was $421,040 for a 1936 Mercedes-Benz Roadster from the M. L. Cohn collection. It was bought by a telephone bidder in Monaco at Christie's sale on February 25, 1979, at the Los Angeles Convention Center.

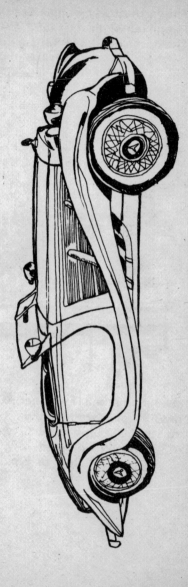

The farthest any woman has thrown a rolling pin (weighing 2 lbs.) is 157 feet 6 inches. Janet Thompson did it at West London Stadium, Wormwood Scrubs, London, England, in 1975.

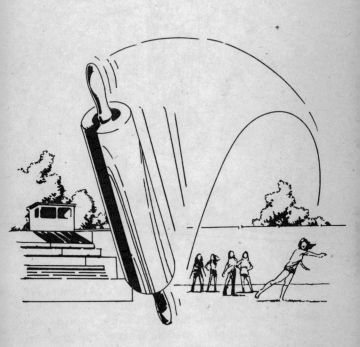

Mark Spitz struck gold in Munich! At the 1972
Olympic Games in Munich, Germany, Mark Spitz
swam in seven races, set seven world records and
collected seven gold medals. This is the greatest
number of gold medals ever won by one person in
a single Olympic Games. He won his medals for
performances in the 100 and 200 meter free-style,
100 and 200 meter butterfly, the 4 x 100 and 4 x 200
free-style relays and the 4 x 100 meter medley relay
(back stroke, breast stroke, butterfly stroke, free-
style).

You can get a musician to play for a party in your living room or your garden, but your pool? Mark Gottlieb is the only violinist to overcome the problems of playing underwater. In March, 1975, he played a submarine version of Handel's "Water Music" in the Evergreen State College swimming pool in Olympia, Washington.

INDEX

air ace, top WWI, 55
aircraft, largest wing span, 26
around-the-world
   first solo flight, 42
   first walk, 43
arrow, longest shot, 31
Aurora Borealis, 28
beauty contest, earliest, 17
bite, strongest, 56
boxing match, shortest, 45
brick-breaker, fastest, 37
bricklayer, fastest, 36
Broadway show, longest running, 25
casting, longest surf, 81
clam, largest, 79
coin balancing, 14
crossword, fastest solution, 82
descent into ocean, deepest, 87
dog litter, largest, 78
driver, fastest woman, 89
driver's test, most failures, 88
eye, largest, 86
fashion show, longest, 53
fire-walk, hottest, 2
fishing
   cast, longest, 81
   marathon, 80
golf
   largest course, 21
   throwing the ball, 20
hairdresser, most durable, 52
hand-milking record, 71
head of state
   longest in office, 32
   oldest, 23
height, greatest difference, 63
hockey player, fastest, 60
horse-racing, long distance, 73
horseshoe pitching marathon, 15
home runs, most, 9
hot water bottle, inflating, 57
hypochondriac, greatest, 18
island, most remote, 69
kangaroo, highest jump, 70
landing from space, most accurate, 49
lawsuit, longest, 13
lawyer, highest-paid, 51
load moved, greatest, 10
migration, longest, 27

milking by hand, 71
music, longest rendition, 66
newspaper, largest, 47
Olympic gold medals, most, 94
pancake, largest flipped, 75
"panning" gold, fastest, 83
pitcher, longest career, 61
prison, largest, 11
professor, longest tenure, 35
pyramid, largest, 50
records
   classic million-seller, 76
   greatest-selling, 77
   greatest-selling artist, 67
reign, longest, 33
rocket, first liquid-fuelled, 48
roll, ultimate ship, 41
roller skate, longest, 72
rolling pin, longest throw, 93
runner, fastest woman, 84
salami, largest, 24
sea voyage, longest, 68
singing marathon, 59
skiing
   greatest altitude, 85
   highest speed, 65
   hot-dog, 64
slide rule, largest, 74
speaker, fastest, 54
spider web, largest, 29
standing longest, 12
swallowing foreign objects, 19
swim, longest, 7
tennis match, longest, 8
tongue-twister, most difficult, 34
"treading" water, longest, 6
treasure hunter, most successful, 30
tug o'war, longest, 44
typed numbers to million, 91
used car, most expensive, 92
violin, played underwater, 95
vocal range, greatest, 58
waterspout, tallest, 39
wave, tallest, 40
weight loss, fastest, 16
well, deepest, 38
wig, longest, 62
worm, longest, 46
writer, least successful published, 90